Melody ♪ Lyrics ♫ Chords

VOLUME ONE

bollywood
classics

Music transcribed and arranged by Leon de Souza

Music from 6 Movies
Piano Vocal Selections

ISBN : 978-1-78038-741-3

 MUSIC SALES
FURTADOS (INDIA) PVT LTD

Published 2012 © Music Sales Furtados (India) Pvt Ltd
International copyright secured. All rights reserved.

Visit Music Sales Furtados at
www.furtadosonline.com

Leon de Souza

Leon de Souza is a Fellow of Trinity College London. In February 1964, he was awarded a scholarship to the Eastman School of Music at the University of Rochester, New York, by Orazio Frugoni. Thus began his long and accomplished career as a musician, teacher, composer and arranger.

As well as being an outstanding accompanist (in any genre from classical music to pop), Leon has composed and recorded numerous jingles and backing tracks, and has also written music for many stage musicals.

Order No. MSF101
ISBN 978-1-78038-741-3

Music transcribed and arranged by Leon de Souza.
Music processed by Paul Ewers Music Design.
Music edited by Tom Farncombe and Ruth Power.
Design by Gina Lobo | SAGI Design
Published by Music Sales Furtados (India) Pvt Ltd

With special thanks to Achille Forler.

Printed in India

Exclusive Distributor in India:
L M Furtado & Co
540- 544, Kalbadevi Road
Mumbai - 400002, INDIA
Tel: +91-22-66225454 | +91-22-22013105
Fax: +91-22-22058750
www.furtadosonline.com

Exclusive Distributor (rest of the world):
Music Sales Limited
Distribution Centre
Newmarket Road
Bury St Edmunds
Suffolk
IP33 3YB, UK
www.musicsales.com

contents

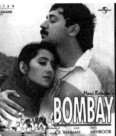

composers and lyricists

A R Rahman

Described as the world's most prominent and prolific film composer by *Time* magazine, A R Rahman's works are notable for integrating eastern classical music with electronic music sounds, world music genres and traditional orchestral arrangements. In 2009, *Time* placed Rahman in its list of The World's Most Influential People. The UK based World Music magazine, *Songlines*, named him as one of 'Tomorrow's World Music Icons' in August 2011. Working in India's various film industries, international cinema and theatre, Rahman has garnered particular acclaim for redefining contemporary Indian film music.

Anu Malik

Son of veteran music director Sardar Malik, Anu Malik made his debut as a music composer in 1977. After a considerable period of struggle, the 90's welcomed Anu with hits like *Phir Teri Kahani Yaad Aayee, Baazigar, Jaanam* and many more. He is one of the most versatile Indian music directors, creating music for almost all kinds of films, without being repetitive, which is said to be the reason for his success. Another specialty of Anu Malik is his choice of singers and lyricists.

Indivar

Indivar is credited with writing some of the finest Bollywood lyrics. He got his first break in *Malhaar* in 1956 and there was no looking back for him after that. In a career spanning four decades this famous Bollywood lyricist has written the lyrics for almost 300 films.

Ismail Darbar

Ismail Darbar hails from a family of four generations of musicians and was introduced to music by his father, who trained him and taught him to play the violin. He worked for nine years as a session violinist for prominent music directors and got his opportunity to compose music when singer Kunal Ganjawala recommended him to director Sanjay Leela Bhansali. Today, he is one of the most highly acclaimed music composers in the industry.

Jatin–Lalit

Jatin-Lalit are a musical duo, who began their music career in 1992. Their composition was influenced by the legendary R D Burman's music style. Despite their success, Jatin-Lalit have generally kept a low profile. However their fans got a chance to see them when they appeared as judges on Zee TV's musical reality show *Sa Re Ga Ma Pa Challenge 2005*. Later they also judged Star Plus's musical show *Star Voice of India*.

Kalyanji – Anandji

Kalyanji-Anandji are a legendary composer duo and are particularly renowned for their work on action movies of the 1970s. Kalyanji and Anandji worked together for more than 400 films. They were known for their modesty and humility, contributing generously to social and charitable causes, and creating opportunities for new talents.

Majrooh Sultanpuri

Majrooh Sultanpuri (1919–2000) belonged to that time in Hindi cinema when films were successful at the box office not only for the story, star cast or direction, but also for their wonderful music and lyrics. He had an illustrious career which spanned over five decades, writing lyrics for almost 350 films, most of which were very popular and broke box office records. He worked with all the top music directors of the time, including Anil Biswas, Naushad, Madan Mohan, O P Nayyar, Roshan and Laxmikant Pyarelal, and also enjoyed particularly fruitful collaborations with S D Burman and R D Burman.

Mehboob

Mehboob Alam Kotwal was born in the village of Chindwara (in the Nashik district of Maharashtra). His family moved to the city of Mumbai for good in the 1940s where he received his primary education, first in English and later in Urdu. In 1986, Mehboob met composer Ismail Darbar, who taught him the difference between poetry and film lyrics. Darbar introduced Mehboob to film-maker Ram Gopal Varma, and he began his songwriting career with Varma's 1992 film *Drohi* the score of which was composed by R D Burman.

Nusrat Badr

Nusrat Badr is an Urdu poet and one of the most under-utilised lyricists in the Hindi film industry, where he debuted with Sanjay Leela Bhansali's *Devdas*.

Rahat Indori

Rahat Indori started teaching Urdu literature in IK College, Indore, and, according to his students, he was the best lecturer in the college. In between, he became very busy with Mushairas and started receiving invitations from all over India and abroad. He became very popular among the masses as well as the classes with his ability, hard work and a characteristic style of delivering Ashaar. He made a place for himself in the hearts of people and within three or four years the style of his poetry had made him a well-known figure in the world of Urdu literature.

Sameer

Sameer is one of the most versatile lyricists in Bollywood. Sameer believes it is important to engage the next generation of audiences, and targets his music at young people. He has written more than 4000 songs for 500 Hindi films to date in a career that has spanned 25 years in Bollywood.

Kehna Hi Kya

from *Mani Ratnam's* **Bombay**
music by **A R Rahman**
lyrics by **Mehboob**

arranged by **Leon de Souza**

Lightly and with rhythm (♩ = 120)

Chorus 1

8

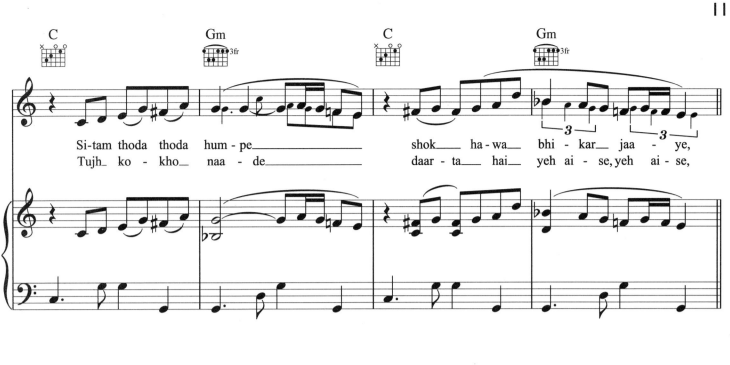

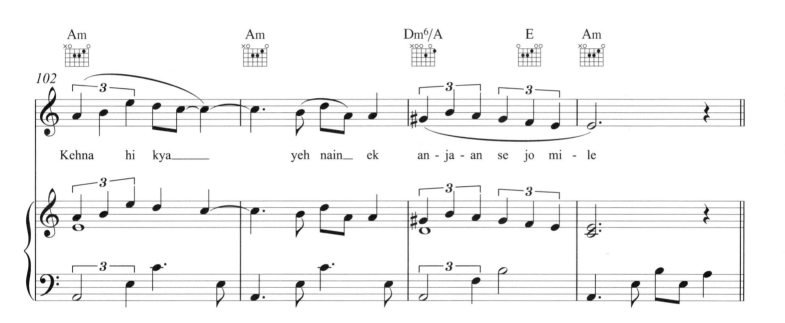

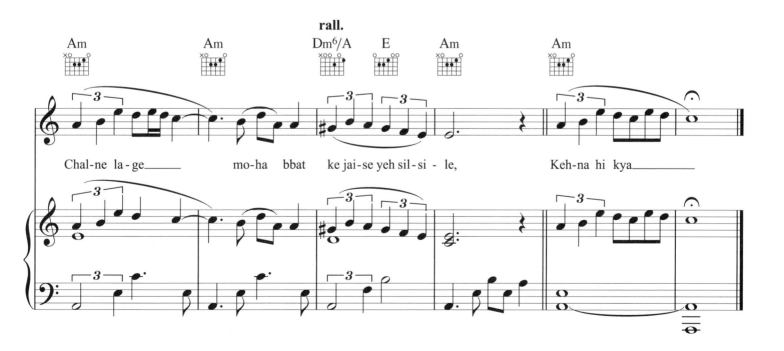

Tu Hi Re

from *Mani Ratnam's* **Bombay**
music by **A R Rahman**
lyrics by **Mehboob**

arranged by **Leon de Souza**

Ik aan-kh ro-ye to du-ji bo - lo,___ so-ye-gi kai - se bha - la, I - n

pya-ar ki raa-hon mein patt-har hain ki-t-ne___ un sab ko hi paar ki - ya, Ek na-

-di hoon main chaa-hat bha-ri aa-j mi-l-ne___ saa-gar ko aa-yi ya-haan, Sa-j-

Chori Chori Chupke Chupke

from *Abbas Mustan's* **Chori Chori Chupke Chupke**
music by **Anu Malik**
lyrics by **Sameer**

arranged by **Leon de Souza**

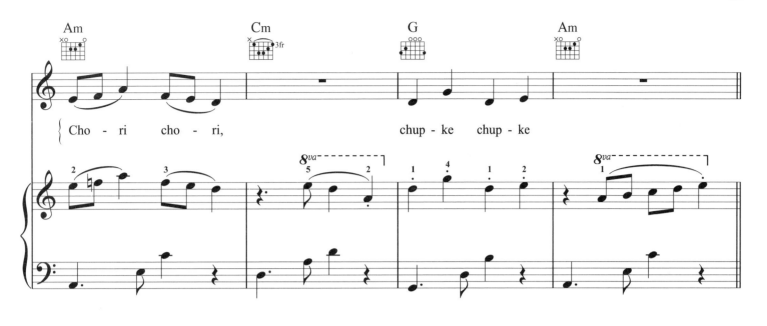

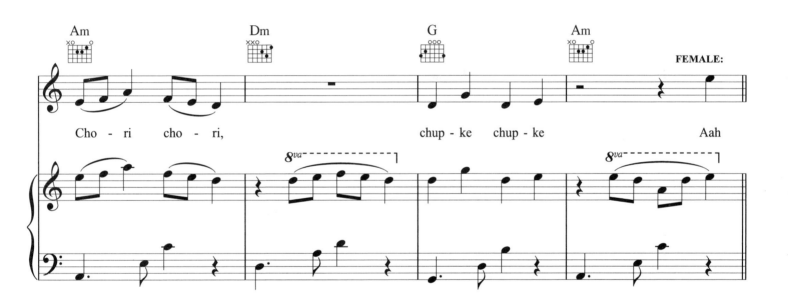

cho - ri cho - ri, chup - ke chup - ke.

MALE:

Cho - ri cho - ri chup - ke chup - ke.

FEMALE:

Cho - ri cho - ri, chup - ke chup - ke.

Silsila Ye Chaahat Ka

from *Sanjay Leela Bhansali's* **Devdas**
music by **Ismail Darbar**
lyrics by **Nusrat Badr**

arranged by **Leon de Souza**

With a joyful and rhythmic feel (♩ = 140)

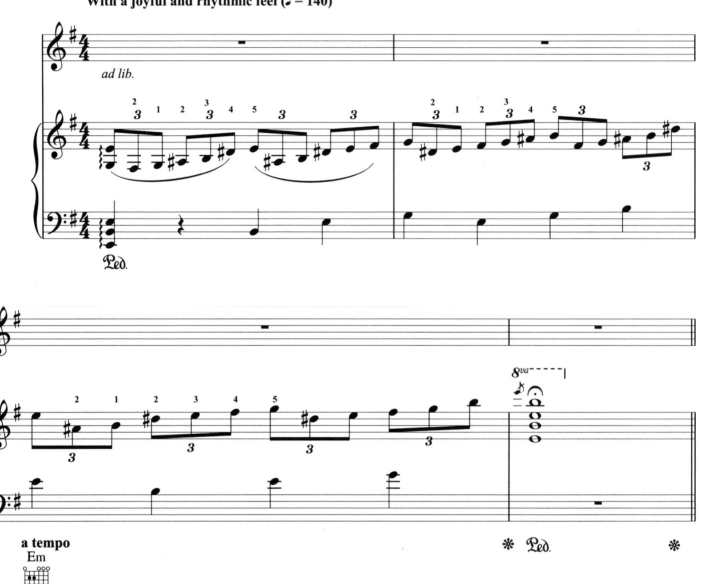

a tempo

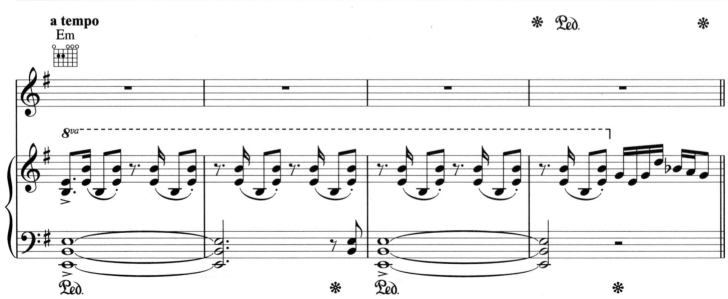

Em
De - kho yeh pag li dee - wa ni, du - ni - ya se hai yeh an - jaa - ni
Jhon - ka ha - wa ka aa ye ga aur is ka pi - ya sang laa ye - ga, Oh pi -
C/E
Em
- ya ab aa - ja re me - re pi - ya,
Sil - si - la yeh chaa - hat ka, na dil se bujh - ne di ya, oh pi -
3

Tera Saath Hai Kitna Pyara

from *Feroz Khan's* **Janbaaz**
music by **Kalyanji-Anandji**
lyrics by **Indivar**

arranged by **Leon de Souza**

Aaj Mai Upar

from *Sanjay Leela Bhansali's* **Khamoshi - The Musical**
music by **Jatin-Lalit**
lyrics by **Majrooh Sultanpuri**

arranged by **Leon de Souza**

With a strong reggae feel (♩ = 192)

62

64

Baahon Ke Darmiyaan

from *Sanjay Leela Bhansali's* **Khamoshi - The Musical**
music by **Jatin-Lalit**
lyrics by **Majrooh Sultanpuri**

arranged by **Leon de Souza**

With much emotion (♩ = 110)

Baa - hon ke dar - mi - yaan,

Do pyaar mil__ ra - he_____ hain,

72

Mausam Ke Sargam

from *Sanjay Leela Bhansali's* **Khamoshi - The Musical**
music by **Jatin-Lalit**
lyrics by **Majrooh Sultanpuri**

arranged by **Leon de Souza**

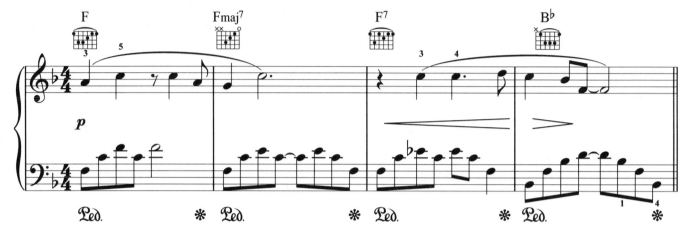

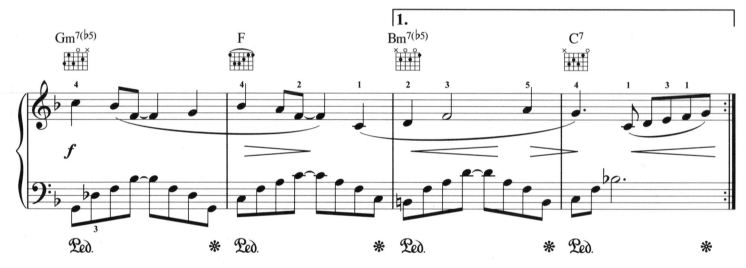

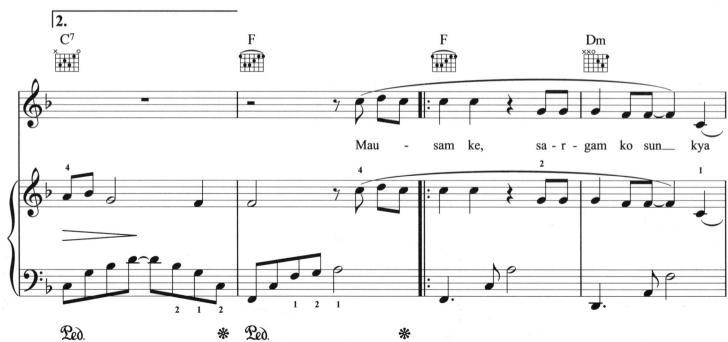

Mau - sam ke, sa - r - gam ko sun__ kya

Yeh Dil Sun Raha Hai

from *Sanjay Leela Bhansali's* **Khamoshi - The Musical**
music by **Jatin-Lalit**
lyrics by **Majrooh Sultanpuri**

arranged by **Leon de Souza**

Chhann Chhann

from *Rajkumar Hirani's* **Munabhai MBBS**
music by **Anu Malik**
lyrics by **Rahat Indori**

arranged by **Leon de Souza**

Lightly and rhythmically (♩ = 160)

106

ga - ye kyun_____

ni sa ni sa   ni sa ni sa

Aah_____

rall.